Bass Book

One

by Cassia Harvey

edited by Nora A. Przybylowski

CHP245

©2013 by C. Harvey Publications All Rights Reserved.
6403 N. 6th Street
Philadelphia, PA 19126
www.charveypublications.com

1. A, B, and C#

Cassia Harvey
edited by Nora A. Przybylowski

2. The Ladybug: A Hungarian Folk Song

3. A, B, C#, and D

Half Notes get 2 counts!

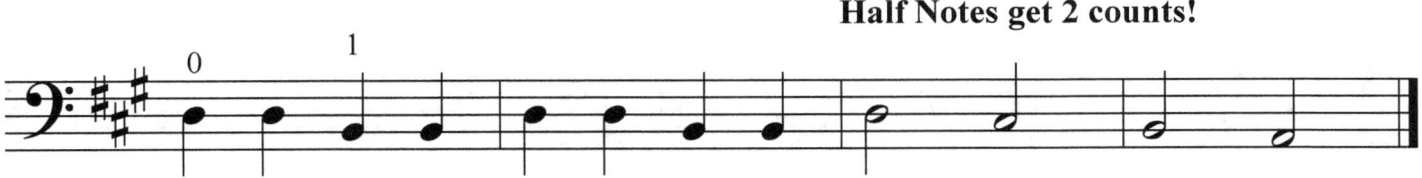

4. By Our Gates: A Russian Folk Song

5. Skipping Around

6. Contredanse: A Danish Folk Song

7. Strengthening the 4th Finger

8. Fiddle Tune

6

An intermediate version of this piece (for more advanced students to play) is on p.32.

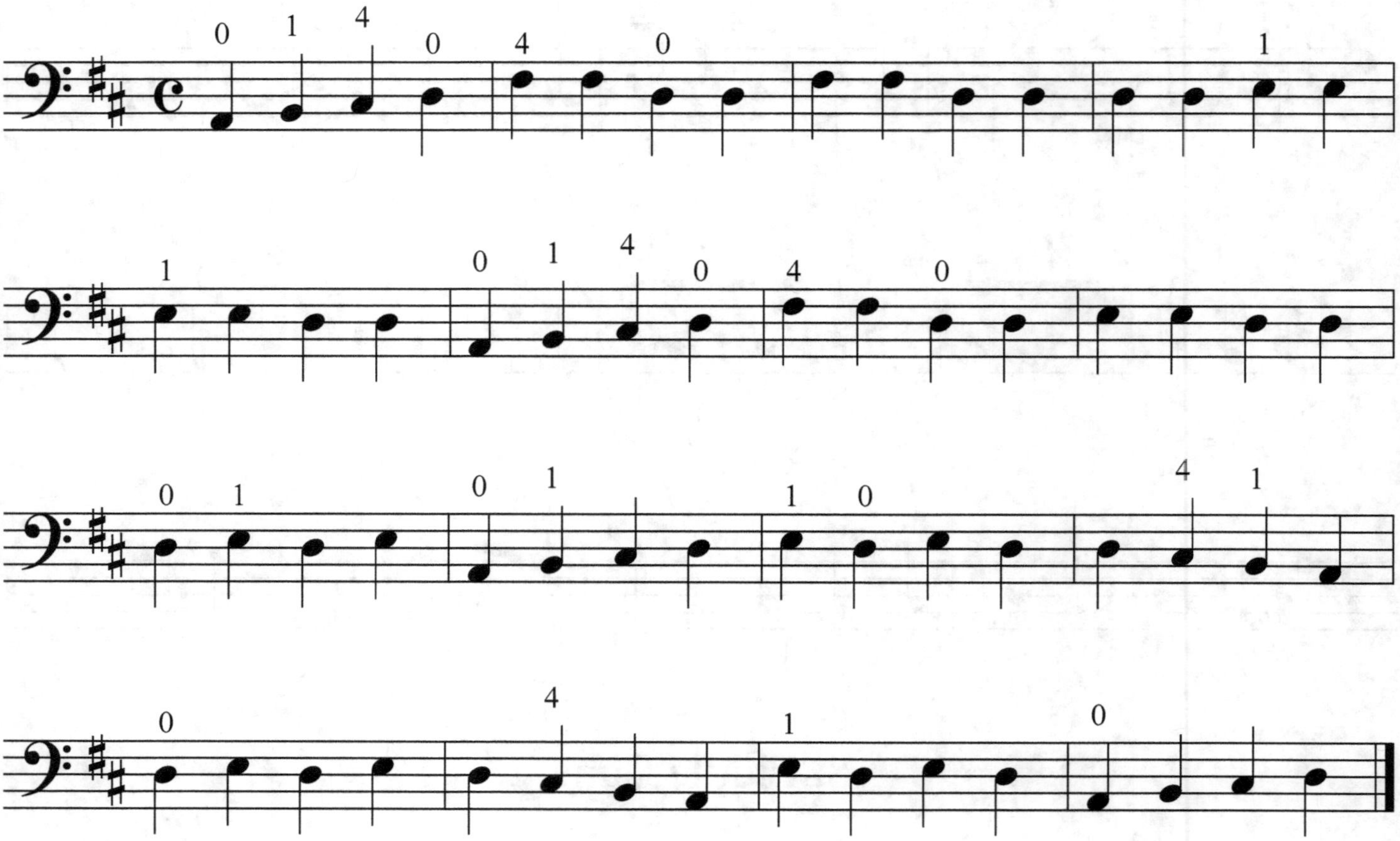

9. Finger Training

10. String Crossing

©2016 C. Harvey Publications All Rights Reserved.

Bass Book One

11. March

An intermediate version of this piece (for more advanced students to play) is on p.32.

12. Polly Wolly Doodle: An American Folk Song

©2016 C. Harvey Publications All Rights Reserved.

An intermediate version of this piece (for more advanced students to play) is on p.33.

13. More Notes

14. Crossing Strings

©2016 C. Harvey Publications All Rights Reserved.

15. The Bold Soldier: A Traditional Folk Song

An intermediate version of this piece (for more advanced students to play) is on p.33.

16. Johnny's Gone for a Soldier: An American Folk Song
(play 2 times)

©2016 C. Harvey Publications All Rights Reserved.

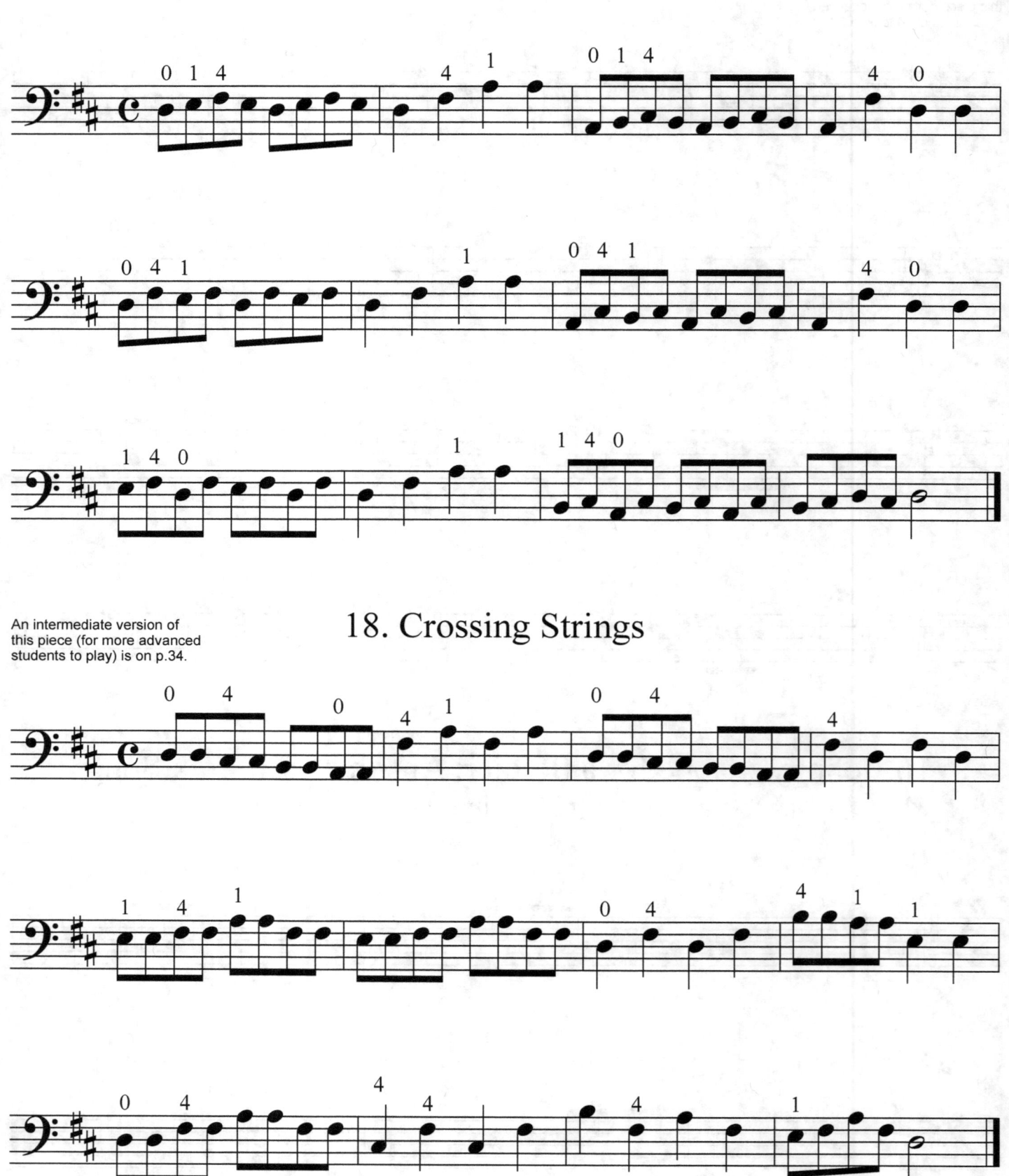

Bass Book One

An intermediate version of this piece (for more advanced students to play) is on p.34.

19. Jasmine Flower: A Chinese Folk Song

20. Tibetan Dance

Dotted half notes get 3 counts!

(slow bow)

©2016 C. Harvey Publications All Rights Reserved.

21. Crossing Strings

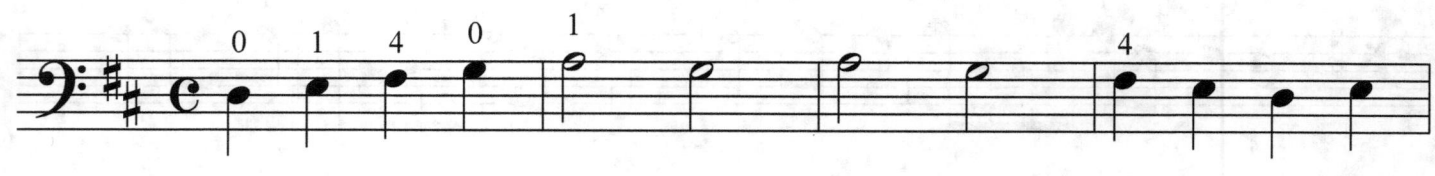
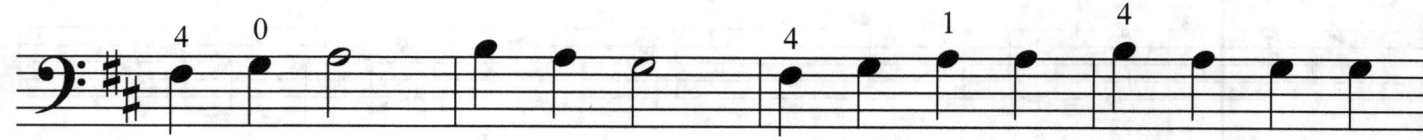

An intermediate version of this piece (for more advanced students to play) is on p.36.

22. More Crossing Strings

©2016 C. Harvey Publications All Rights Reserved.

Bass Book One

An intermediate version of this piece (for more advanced students to play) is on p.36.

23. Crowninshield's Mother Goose

24. Crossing Strings and Skipping Notes

An intermediate version of this piece (for more advanced students to play) is on p.37.

25. Bowing Practice

Bass Book One

26. Chinese Folk Song

27. Theme from Schubert's "The Trout"

©2016 C. Harvey Publications All Rights Reserved.

28. Exercise to Focus on the D String

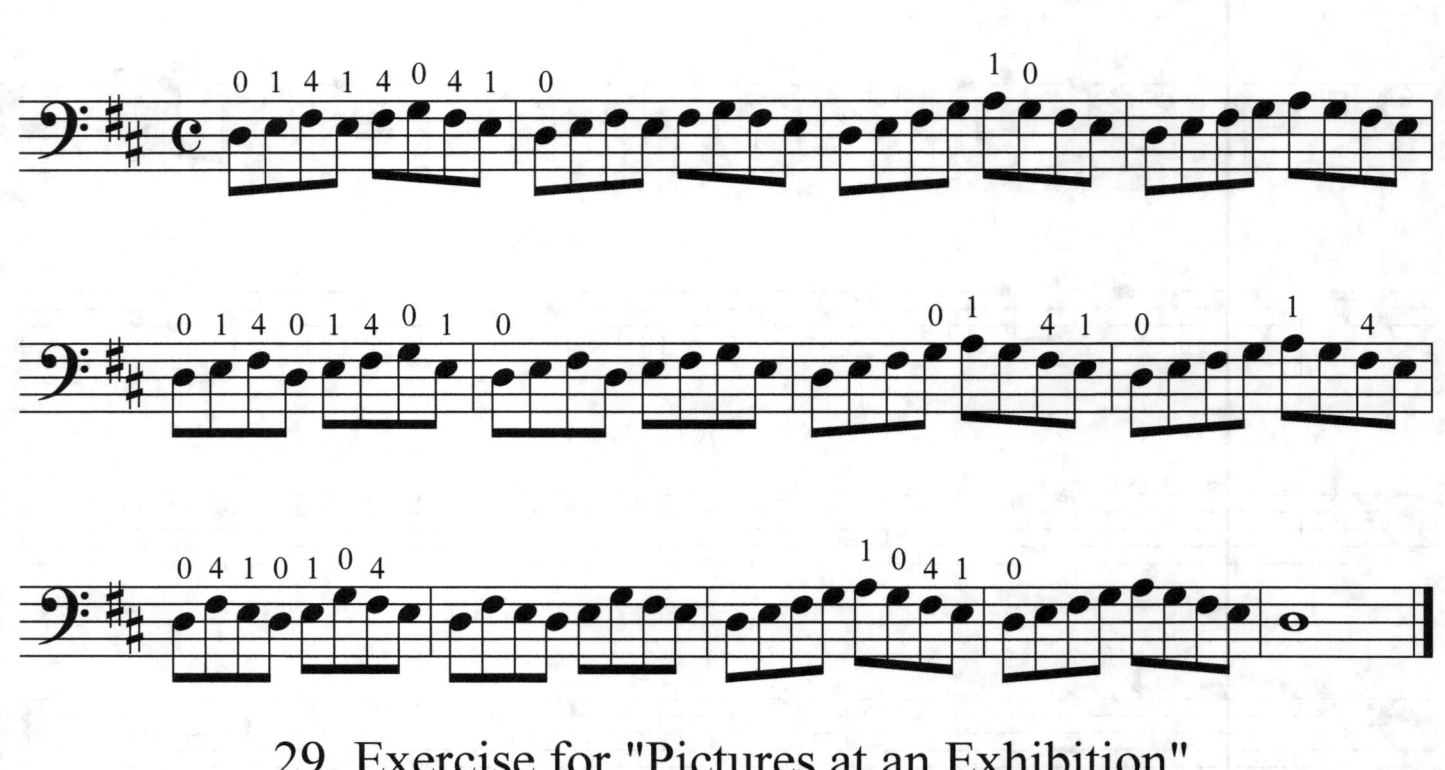

29. Exercise for "Pictures at an Exhibition"

An intermediate version of this piece (for more advanced students to play) is on p.38.

30. Waltz by Alexandrov

31. Theme from Mussorgsky's "Pictures at an Exhibition"

An intermediate version of this piece (for more advanced students to play) is on p. 38.

An intermediate version of this piece (for more advanced students to play) is on p.39.

32. Second Finger C♮

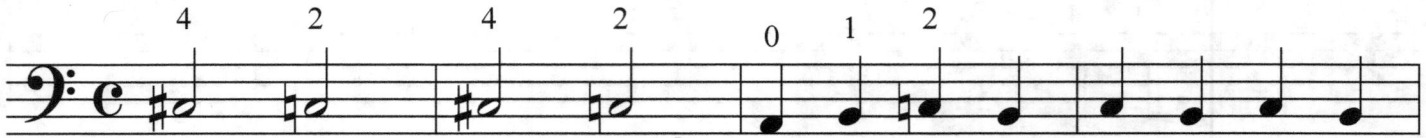

33. Second Finger F♮

©2016 C. Harvey Publications All Rights Reserved.

Bass Book One

34. Spanish Minuet

An intermediate version of this piece (for more advanced students to play) is on p.39.

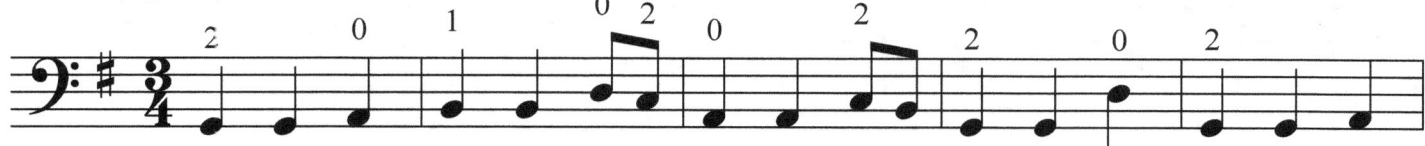

35. Donizetti's Theme from L'Elisir D'Amor

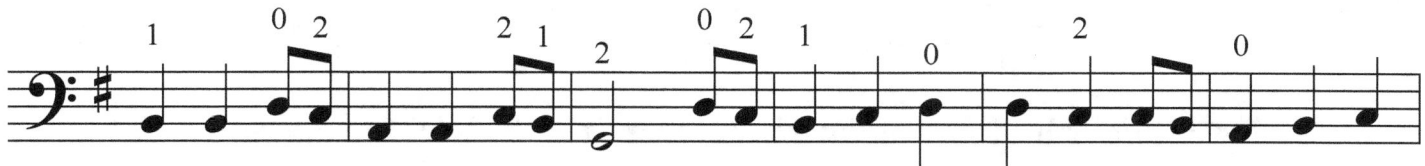

©2016 C. Harvey Publications All Rights Reserved.

20 An intermediate version of this piece (for more advanced students to play) is on p.40.

36. Using 2nd Finger on A and 4th Finger on D

37. Fourth Finger on D: There is an F# in the Key Signature!

38. On the G String

©2016 C. Harvey Publications All Rights Reserved.

Bass Book One

39. Dance from Tchaikovsky's Swan Lake

An intermediate version of this piece (for more advanced students to play) is on p.40.

©2016 C. Harvey Publications All Rights Reserved.

40. Lower Notes
(Cellos Learn G String)

41. Crossing Strings

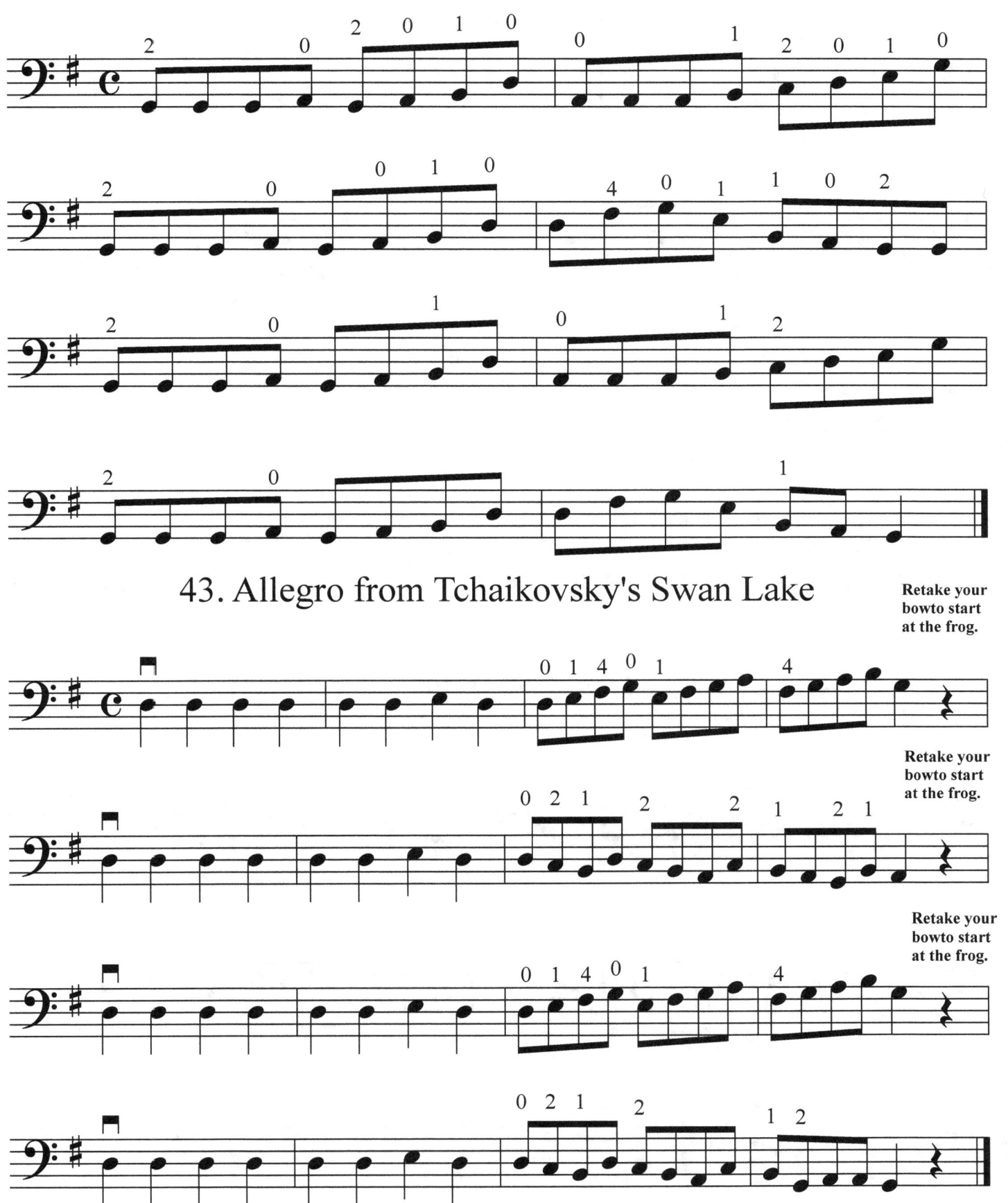

44. Lower Notes

45. Skipping

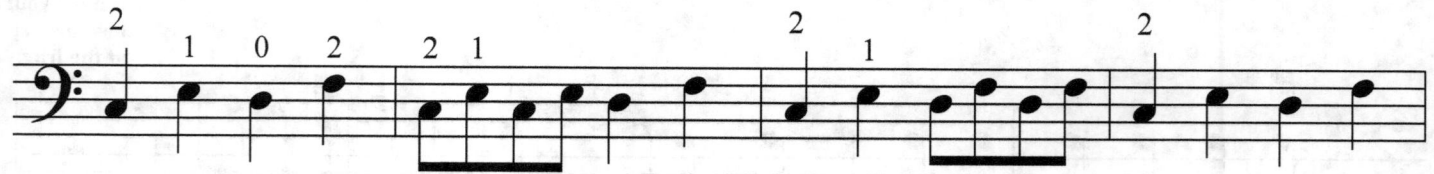

46. Theme from Rimsky-Korsakov's Scheherazade

47. Ballet Music from Schubert's Rosamunde

Bass Book One
27

50. Theme from Mahler's First Symphony

51. Galopade, by Glinka

An intermediate version of this piece (for more advanced students to play) is on p.42.

©2016 C. Harvey Publications All Rights Reserved.

52. Sliding Back to Low 1st Finger

28

An intermediate version of this piece (for more advanced students to play) is on p.43.

Bass Book One

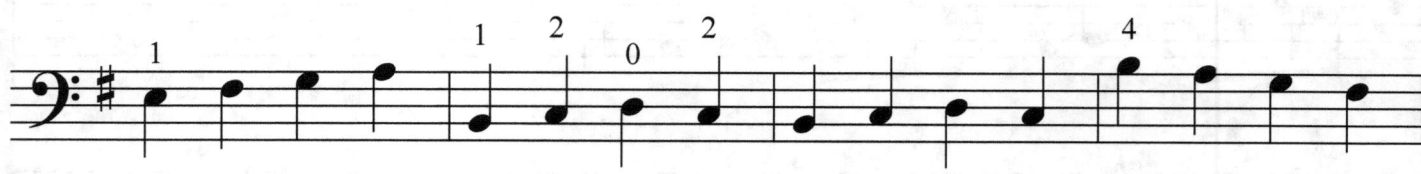

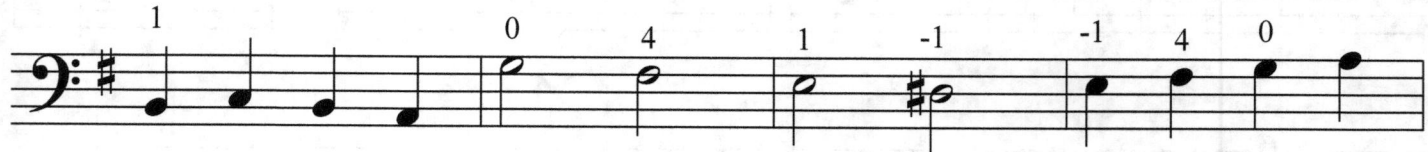

©2016 C. Harvey Publications All Rights Reserved.

Bass Book One

53. I Went to Sea for Oranges: A Spanish Folk Song

54. Mozart's Alleluia

An intermediate version of this piece (for more advanced students to play) is on p.44.

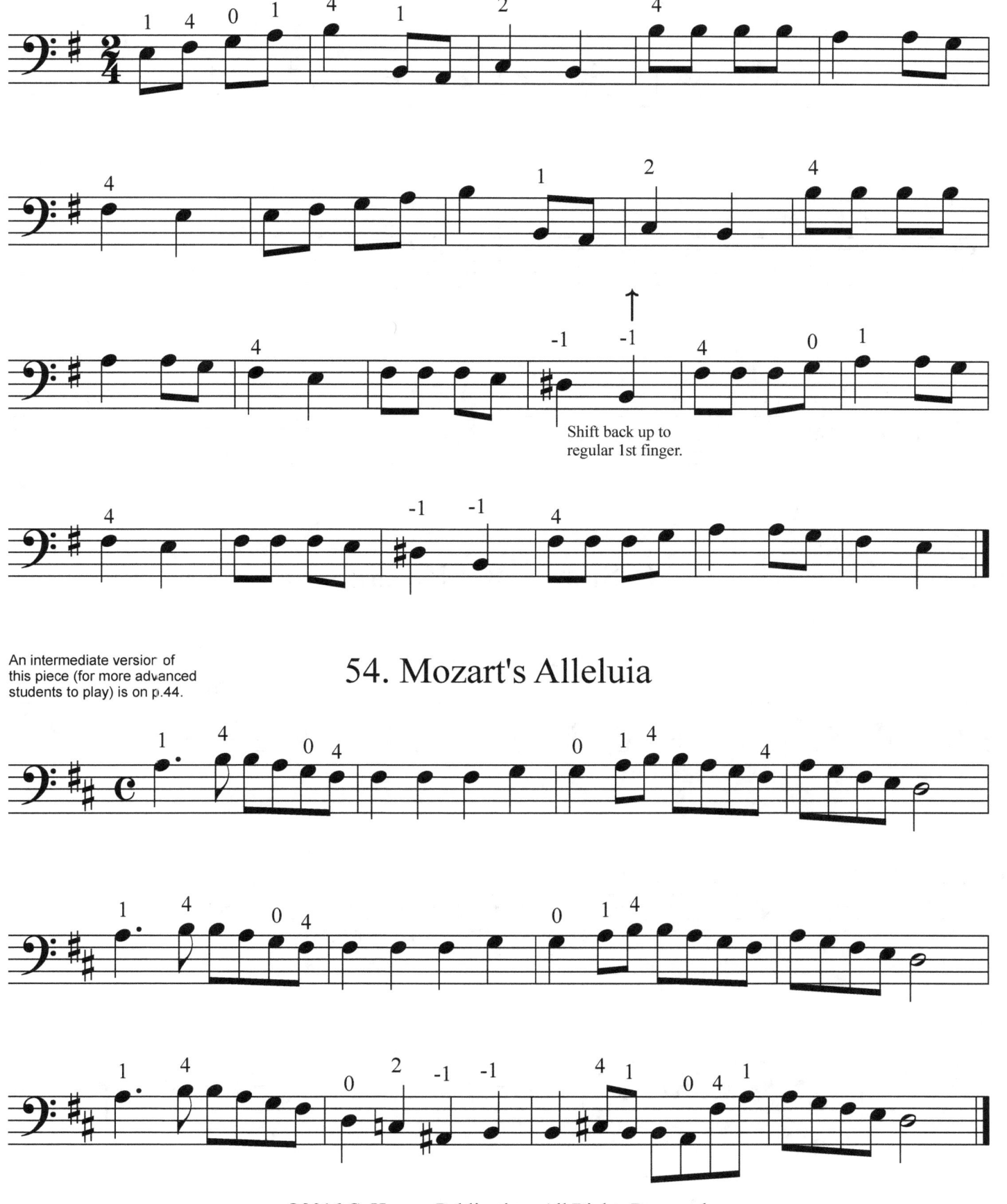

©2016 C. Harvey Publications All Rights Reserved.

55. Reviewing Sharps

56. Sharps and Naturals

Bass Book One

57. Theme from Beethoven's Symphony No. 6

58. Cotton-Eyed Joe: A Fiddle Tune

An intermediate version of this piece (for more advanced students to play) is on p.44.

©2016 C. Harvey Publications All Rights Reserved.

Advanced Versions of Selections from Bass Book One

9. Finger Training

11. March

©2016 C. Harvey Publications All Rights Reserved.

Bass Book One

13. More Notes

15. The Bold Soldier

18. Crossing Strings to Third Finger

19. Jasmine Flower: A Chinese Folk Song

This page left blank to help with page turns.

22. More Crossing Strings

23. Crowninshield's Mother Goose

Bass Book One

24. Crossing Strings and Skipping Notes

29. Exercise for "Pictures at an Exhibition"

31. Theme from Mussorgsky's "Pictures at an Exhibition"

32. C♮

34. Spanish Minuet

36. C♮ and F♯

39. Dance from Tchaikovsky's Swan Lake

Bass Book One

49. Review Exercise

51. Galopade, by Glinka

52. Sliding Back to Half Position

54. Mozart's Alleluia

58. Cotton-Eyed Joe: A Fiddle Tune

www.ingramcontent.com/pod-product-compliance
Lightning Source LLC
Chambersburg PA
CBHW051426070526
44584CB00023B/3599